DO THE RIGHT THING!

MANNERS

Written by Eric Suben
Illustrated by Barbara Lanza

ROURKE BOOK CO., INC.
VERO BEACH, FL 32964

Printed in the United States of America.

Library of Congress Cataloging-in-Publication Data

Suben, Eric.
   Manners / Eric Suben.
      p.   cm. — (Doing the right thing)
Summary: Presents examples of showing good manners in school, play, the movies, and other situations.
   ISBN 1-55916-234-1
   1. Children—Conduct of life. 2. Etiquette for children and teenagers.   [1. Etiquette.]   I. Title.
II. Series.
BJ1631.S93   1999
395.1'22—dc21

                                     98-48388
                                         CIP
                                         AC

MANNERS

4

If you have good manners, people will call you polite, well-behaved, thoughtful, and kind.

5

Having manners means doing nice things for
people in a nice way. You say, "Good morning!"
with a cheerful smile.

You eat your breakfast and drink
your milk without leaving a mess.

If you get to the school bus on time, the other children will not have to wait for you. That is good manners.

9

Raise your hand before speaking out loud in class. Call your teacher by name instead of yelling, "Hey!" It is polite to keep quiet when someone else is speaking.

Waiting your turn when you are
playing a game is good manners .

Say "please" when you want something.
Say "thank you" after you are given something.

Having good manners means trying to help people wherever you are. Sometimes you can help by holding the door.

14

Sometimes you can help by picking up
something that has been dropped.
"Excuse me," is the polite thing to say
if you are in the way.

Show your good manners by saying, "Hello!"
to your friend's family when you go to play
at her house. Thank your friend's parents
for letting you come to play.

It is polite to help clean up after
you have finished playing.

Good manners are important at home, too.
Ask if you can help set the table for supper.
Try to be quiet without being asked.

Wash your hands before you sit down to eat.

Sit up straight at the dinner table.
You are not a baby anymore!

When you are seated at the dinner table, ask people whether they would like something before taking some yourself. It is *not* good manners to stick your hands in the mashed potatoes!

Good manners are used everywhere You can
run around and make noise at the park, but
look out for others and don't get too loud.

Running around and making noise *would not*
be good manners at the movies! Sitting still
and being quiet is the best behavior there.

Manners may be different with different people. It is good manners to shake hands with Dad's boss.

It is good manners to give Grandma
a great, big hug.

Sometimes your parents want you to be on your best behavior. Help make company feel at home.

You can do that by asking guests to come inside and by taking their coats.

Your parents will thank you if you are very
well behaved when you go out. Your napkin
belongs in your lap. Remember to eat neatly.

Show your good manners at a party.
Thank your hostess for inviting you.
Greet your friends. When you play a
game wait your turn and don't make
too much noise.

Help clean up, and remember, say "thank you" again before you go home. You can have good manners and have fun, too!

You Can Have Manners!

These steps can help you have good manners. But do NOT write in this book; use a sheet a paper.

1. Do you have any good manners now? If you do, write 5 of them.
>   I am cheerful.
>   I wait my turn when I play games.
>   I say "excuse me" if I bump into someone.
>   I look at a person who talks to me.
>   I chew food with my mouth closed.

2. Do you have any bad manners now? If you do, write 3 of them.
>   I don't cover my mouth when I cough.
>   I'm grumpy if I get beat in a game.
>   I talk too loud in the library and restaurants.

3. How can you change bad manners? Write 2 ways for each of your bad manners.
>   I talk too loud ...
>>   Pretend I'm a spy looking for clues.
>>   See how low I can talk and still be heard.

4. Start now. Pick one way to change today.

5. Start each day right. Use good manners first thing every morning.

6. Write these words every evening:
>   Today I had good manners when I _____.

Fill in the blank. Use the same paper every time. Keep it up for 2 weeks or more.

7. Say, "I have good manners."
>   Say it many times each day.

32